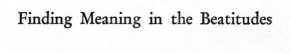

Finding Meaning in the Beatitudes

Finding Meaning
in the Beatitudes

John A. Redhead

ℐ

ABINGDON PRESS
Nashville and New York

To
Anna, Julia, and Mary Lauchlin
Elizabeth and Virginia

Contents

1.   Blessed Are the Poor in Spirit

"Blessed are the poor in spirit, for theirs is the kingdom of heaven."—Matthew 5:3

Down in southern Mississippi there are several kinds of trees from which we gathered nuts in the fall. Among them were pecan trees and walnut trees. The black walnut has a shell which is hard to crack, but its meat is the best. It is so with certain verses in the Bible: the harder they are to crack, the sweeter the kernel within.

It is so with the words which form our topic. There are ten books on my shelves which attempt to explain them. I read through nine of them and felt I was on a cold trail. If nine had failed, why try the tenth? That night I took the first beatitude to bed with me and slept on it, but it still seemed as far from reality as possible. Next morning I opened the tenth book, and then the light broke: here at last was an insight which linked these words with life. What Jesus said is this: "Blessed

are the poor in spirit, for theirs is the kingdom
of heaven." What did he mean, and how can you
find the happiness of which he spoke?

I

Take, first of all, his words "poor in spirit." It
is plain there is one thing he did not mean. He did
not say, for example, "Blessed are the poor-
spirited." That is a misconception of the Christian
life which sometimes gets hold of us. We think of
someone who is helpless and dejected, who seems
to think crawling is the Christian's proper gait.
He has no spirit left in him and is afraid to call
his soul his own. He will not hold his head up and
seems not to wish to be master of this thing
called life. There is no red blood in his body, and
his backbone is made out of spaghetti. His morale
is run down at the heels. He allows circumstances
to get the better of him and wears his defeat in
his face. He seems to think it is a virtue to allow
others to run over him. He baptizes his cowardice
with holy water and calls it humility. That is the
kind of man we usually think of as being "poor
in spirit." But that is not Christianity: it is only
creeping paralysis.

If you doubt that, you have only to think of
our Lord and his effect upon men. Some artists

have painted him with a face which makes him look like a man who has lost his last friend, and such paintings have gone a long way toward giving the wrong impression. In a college bull session someone asked the question, Who is the most Christlike man in school? I thought of a student who always wore this look of somber dejection and gave his name.

But I was glad to learn later that I was wrong. I remembered that no picture we have of Christ was painted by anybody who ever saw him. The portraits we have were painted centuries after his death, and many were made at a time when the ascetic was the ideal Christian life. That means that there came a time in the church's history when life was so worldly that the leaders sought to escape from it by mortification of the flesh. What you see when you look at one of these paintings is not the real Christ at all, but what the men who lived years later thought he looked like. ʃThe Christ who walks up and down the pages of the New Testament was a long way from being poor-spirited. He said he had overcome the world and he had, and he inspired such a red-blooded courage in men like Simon Peter and the apostle Paul and their like that they went out to face a power like the Roman Empire and turned it upside down—just as some of his present-day disciples

11

are turning our contemporary society upside down. "Poor in spirit" does not mean, of all things, poor-spirited. What then does it mean?

We can get closer to our Lord's meaning if we substitute for the word "spirit" our more modern word "ego." Ego means self, and to be rich in ego is to have too much of the same. We know people who are rich in ego, and we do not like them. They are proud and haughty and conceited. They have an overweening sense of their own importance. Those who are rich in ego are the self-satisfied, the self-sufficient, the self-seeking, and the self-centered. Says a contemporary novelist about one of her characters: "Edith was a little country bounded on the north, south, east, and west by Edith." To be rich in ego is to be self-contained. It is to possess such an acute awareness of self that one's world begins and ends with self.

Some months ago, when I was thinking about this first beatitude, there was an article on the sports page of one of our papers. It was about Art Heyman, when he was playing basketball at Duke University, and it quoted him as saying that he had grown up a lot in his four years there. "When I came to Duke," he said, "I was a brash, hot-tempered seventeen-year-old. I had been offered over a hundred scholarships and felt a little big. . . . Then I began to face reality. With the help of coaches Vic Bubas and Fred Shabel I began to grow up . . . and I learned to become humble."

That is what it means to be poor in spirit. It is not to feel big but to be humble. It is not to be self-seeking, but self-renouncing. It is not to be self-centered, but self-circumferenced. It is a thirsty land crying out for rain. It is Bill Bradley of Princeton, passing off to his teammates, so they may make goals and get the credit. It is a congregation singing "I Need Thee Every Hour." It is the publican, beating upon his breast and crying out, "God, be merciful to me a sinner!" (Luke 18:13). It is Jesus on his knees in the Garden, praying, "Not my will, but thine" (Luke 22:42). It is any man, and every man, who has so completely got rid of self as the determining factor in his life that he is willing to issue a declaration of dependence upon a higher power. That is what it means to be poor in spirit.

II

Go on and notice, in the second place, that Jesus tells us the only way to get rid of self is to make room for God. "Blessed are the poor in spirit, for theirs is the kingdom of heaven."

13

"Kingdom of heaven" is another of those phrases like "poor in spirit." It was written originally in the Greek language; and as far as most of us are concerned, it is still Greek to us. But when you break it down, you find it saying something that is real.

These words were written at a time when a ruler was accorded absolute power over his subjects. So it was with the Roman emperor or with a king in his country. Kingdom or kingship meant the exercise of power and authority. The word "heaven," being the name of the place where God resides, came to mean God himself. The Jews had a certain reluctance in repeating the name of deity; and Matthew, writing for the Jews, uses the word "heaven" when he means God. In the New Testament, the kingdom of heaven and the kingdom of God mean the same thing. We use the words in identical manner. We say sometimes "Heaven help us," when what we mean is "God help us." So when Jesus says "Blessed are the poor in spirit, for theirs is the kingdom of heaven," he means "Happy are they who are empty of self, because God rules with full power in their lives."

Sometimes you hear it said of some person, "He is a self-made man, and he worships his maker." That is always the danger with the self-sufficient; but in every life there is a throne and a cross. As long as self is on the throne, God is on the cross.

14

Yet when you walk up to that throne and take self from the seat of authority and place it on the cross, then God can take his place on the throne and rule: then yours is the kingdom of heaven. I heard an old minister pray this prayer once: "O God, help us to be emptied of self that we may be filled with thee." The only way to get rid of too much ego is to make room for God.

III

Go on and note, in the third place, that this poverty of spirit is absolutely essential for any kind of happiness. With self out on the circumference and God at the center, life finds its true center and begins to swing with that grace and rhythm which are free from friction and frustration.

There are three realities with which each of us has to deal, and our happiness depends upon our being properly adjusted to all three.

The first is ourselves, and with self out of the way and God at the center we are free to become properly adjusted. A few years ago there was a best-selling book which had a chapter called "Getting Oneself Off One's Hands." The author tells about a certain charm school which promised to bestow "personality" upon its clients. It pre-scribed in its first lesson that the client stand before a large mirror and repeat his name in a voice "soft, gentle, and low" in order to impress himself with himself. The author goes on to say that turning your attention to yourself may increase obsession with yourself, which is the very thing most sick selves are suffering from. The wisdom of the race has put this truth in the fable of the Frog and the Ox. When the frog sought to blow himself up as big as the ox, he swelled and swelled until he burst. And Aesop does not leave us to draw our own conclusions: "Self-conceit," he says, "may lead to self-destruction."

If you doubt that happiness blows up in the face of a bloated sense of self-importance, you have only to look at it in some of its varied expressions. When you are overly self-conscious in a crowd, you are miserable. You imagine you are the focus of everyone's attention as well as your own, and in a social group you become embarrassed and confused. But what is self-consciousness except too much consciousness of self? When you are overly sensitive, you are made miserable by that too. Your feelings stick out on every side, and someone is always stepping on them. But what is sensitiveness, except an overemphasis on self which demands that everyone accord you the same importance which you attach to yourself? And you who suffer from self-pity, you are unhappy too.

16

You cannot bear to be thwarted, misunderstood, ridiculed, or defeated. But what is self-pity, except the feeling of a person who attaches too much importance to himself and who supposes that his whole world consists in what happens to himself and the way he feels?

"The happiest day of my life," said a certain woman, "was the day I stopped trying to be pretty." She had to let her pretensions about herself go and accept herself for what she was. She had got herself off her hands by becoming poor in spirit.

The second reality with which we have to deal is other people, and our happiness depends upon being properly adjusted not only to ourselves but to them as well.

There is an instinctive desire which everybody has, to enjoy the admiration and esteem of the people with whom he lives. When you enjoy their approval, you are happy, and when you are denied it, you are unhappy. And there is nothing in the world which gets in the way of such approval more quickly than self-centeredness. You can put up with self-centeredness in a child because it is natural to his age; but for an older person to fail to grow out of that selfishness which constantly demands the center of the stage is fatal to his happiness.

17

Ralph W. Sockman has a chapter on this beatitude, and in it is a sentence which describes this person to a T: he says that the only music the self-centered man hears is the blowing of his own horn. Then he goes on to tell about a writer who was talking with a group at a social affair and had been regaling them with a running account of his own activities and achievements. Finally he stopped and said: "Enough about myself. Let's hear from you. What do you think of my latest book?"

Long ago I learned that some people are more interesting in conversation than others. When I got around to asking why, I discovered that the less interesting were so because they were always talking about themselves. A bore is a person, so the story goes, who, when you ask him how he feels, tells you. But if you check on your own experience, you will find that the people you enjoy being with are those who have got themselves out of the way, and as soon as you meet them begin asking about you and your interests.

You can divide people into two groups: those who see life as a mirror and those who see life as a window. For the self-centered person the world is a mirror. Wherever he looks, he sees himself. He is like the person window-shopping who never sees the goods in the window but himself in the glass. But for the poor in spirit, the world is a window: he looks through the glass and sees what is on the other side. And blessed are the poor in spirit, for they are rich in the esteem of a multitude of friends.

The third reality with which we have to deal is God, and our happiness depends upon our being properly adjusted not only to ourselves and to other people, but to God as well.

There is nothing so fatal to this sense of being right with God and enjoying his approval as the self-important assumption that you can win it for yourself. The Apostle tried it and ended by saying: "Wretched man that I am" (Rom. 7:24). Martin Luther tried it and found himself in a like despair. John Wesley tried it, and the failure of his mission to America was symbolic of his failure to find peace with God by working his way to heaven.

And it will be so with any man who claims that he is the master of his fate and the captain of his soul. If he sets out to row his own boat and paddle his own canoe; if he says: "With these two legs of mine I'll climb the steep ascent of heaven, and when I get to the door I'll batter it down with the strong arm of my righteousness, I'll storm the citadel of the Eternal, and demand that God take me in on the basis of my own merit," he is riding for a fall.

The entire history of religion says that if you want the blessedness which comes from being right with God, you have got to get self out of the way. You have got to swallow your pride and be willing to admit that you cannot make the grade under your own steam. You have got to see that it is by grace you are saved. You have got to see that your own check is no good on the bank of heaven: to come and stand before God and say to him:

> Nothing in my hand I bring,
> Simply to Thy cross I cling.

You have got to see with Paul Tillich that our human condition is that we are estranged from God and our only hope lies in the fact that he is willing to "accept the unacceptable." You have got to be *poor* in spirit.

I have heard that in one of the churches in Copenhagen there is an unusual statue of Christ. I do not know what material it is made of; but a story that I read says that after it had been finished by the artist Thorwaldsen, an accident occurred. For some reason, perhaps because of a lack of proper conditions of temperature, the head of the statue bent forward; and it was decided to put it in its place without restoring the head to

20

its normal position. It is there today, with the head bent forward. A visitor to the church saw this unusual statue, and when he asked why the artist would make this kind of creation, he received this answer: "If you want to see his face, you've got to get on your knees."

When you live in the kingdom of self, you will never know the blessedness of the kingdom of heaven, for that is reserved for those who are poor in spirit.

2.   Blessed Are Those Who Mourn

"Blessed are those who mourn, for they shall be comforted."—Matthew 5:4

I had thought that the first beatitude was the hardest nut to crack I had ever seen, but when I came to the second I was really stumped. After days of reading and thinking about it, I was almost at the point of deciding that I couldn't make heads or tails of it and would have to pass it by and go on to the next. I never wished so strongly in my life for a personal conference with Jesus so that I might say to him: "Lord, tell me what you had in mind when you said 'Blessed are they that mourn.'" Then I remembered that he promised his Spirit to be our teacher who would take the things that are his and show them to us. Gradually that promise began to be fulfilled, and I trust his words will make some point of contact in your experience.

I am sure he did not give his consent to the

miserable habit of luxuriating in grief. We all know people who enjoy poor health and revel in their woes. They go around with their faces draped in black, always eager to recite their misfortunes in order to enjoy the morbid pleasure of the soul that is sick with self-pity.

Neither is he denying that there is enjoyment which comes from the good things of life. Happiness is happiness, whether you find it in the plus or whether you are forced to find it in the minus; and when you find it in the plus, Jesus is the last person in the world to deny you the pleasure of enjoying it.

Nor is he saying that the only happiness you can expect comes from having the causes of your unhappiness removed. Had he meant that, he would have said "Blessed are those who mourn, for they shall be consoled." But to be comforted is something different from being consoled, as we shall see.

I

When you set out to discover what he meant, you must begin where he began, with the word "blessed." It has had a history in our language, and its story includes three stages. In its first stage it meant rich: it comes from a word meaning great, and at first this greatness was limited to outward prosperity. Among the Greeks, the man who was blessed or happy was the man who was rich in outward possessions. But one day Croesus called in the counselor Solon and put to him this question: "Who is the happiest man in all the world?" Being the richest, Croesus naturally thought that he himself would be named, but Solon answered: "Call no man happy until he is dead." He did not mean that there is no happiness in life but rather this: If you make happiness depend upon fortunate circumstances, you cannot tell whether anyone is happy until he is dead, until all returns are in and you can balance the plus against the minus.

The second stage in the history of the word "blessed" is represented by the philosophers, when the meaning of happiness rises from outward prosperity to inward virtue. But in all the philosophers this inward virtue depends upon knowledge, so that to be happy was first of all to know. Yet when you limit happiness to knowledge you make it a monopoly of the Ph.D.'s.

The third stage in this history is the biblical stage, which lifts the meaning of happiness into the spiritual, as distinct from the merely intellectual, and which makes happiness depend upon what a man is and not upon what he has. In the

Old Testament this happiness is always attested by outward prosperity which comes from inward righteousness, but in the New Testament the word shakes itself loose from all thought of outward good and becomes a symbol of happiness, identified purely with inward character.

One afternoon several years ago, we boarded a plane in Athens on our way to Jerusalem. The first stop was the city of Nicosia on the island of Cyprus. I remembered that the political ruler of Cyprus is an archbishop of the Orthodox Church, and I was interested to recall later on that his name is the Greek word which means "blessed" in this beatitude: *Makarios.* Furthermore, before Cyprus developed its more recent troubles, it was always known as "the Makaria," which means "the Happy Isle." The Greeks called it that because they believed that Cyprus was so lovely an island that a man would never need to go beyond its coastline to find the perfectly happy life. It has such a climate, such flowers and fruits and trees, such minerals and natural resources, that it was thought to contain all the materials for perfect happiness.

Which thing is a parable. *Makarios,* or blessedness, describes that joy which has its secret within itself. Our word "happiness" gives its case away. Its first three letters are "hap" which means chance; and so human happiness is something which depends upon the chances of life, something which the world can give and which the world can take away. But blessedness is something else. It has its own natural resources and is untouchable. Jesus says, "No one will take your joy from you" (John 16:22). And so the blessedness of which this beatitude speaks is a joy which has its secret within itself.

II

There are three directions in which this truth holds good, and the first is in our relation with ourselves. It has to do with how you deal with the fact of personal loss and grief and sorrow and pain; and it says there is a way of dealing with trouble so that it need not destroy joy.

The problem of pain and suffering is as old as life itself, and the minds of men have attempted four solutions. The first is to deny the reality of suffering, to bury your head in the sand and refuse to see. That is the method of the Christian Scientist. I was talking with such a man once, and when I asked him what he did with the suffering of Jesus on the cross, he used a word I never heard before. He said "I just unsee it." That calls for a mental trick of magic which I have never learned. The second solution is to count suffering an evil and seek to get rid of it by getting rid of the capacity to feel and therefore to suffer. That is the method of the Stoic, and it does violence to your humanity. The third solution is to regard suffering as the result of the will of God and submit to it, with the hope that in the end he will tip the scales in your favor. That is the method of the Mohammedan. The fourth solution is to accept the trouble as a part of life and make something out of it. That is the method of the Christian.

The key word in the Christian solution is the word "accept." That is not easy to do, because when fate sends some

> . . . rebuff
> That turns earth's smoothness rough,

your first reaction is to rebel. You say "My God, my God, why—why should this thing have to happen to me?" And then your rebellion turns to resentment, and you begin to hold a big grudge against God. But so far as I am aware, nowhere is the promise made that this life will be a picnic. On the contrary, Jesus put it as plainly as words can say it: "In the world you have tribulation" (John 16:33)—period! Tribulation means trouble; and what he is saying is that in the kind of world in which you live you might as well take it for

27

granted there will be things you will not like. Yet he did not stop there. He went on to say this: "But be of good cheer, I have overcome the world."

When you begin to look around for some secret which will help you accept and so to overcome your trouble, you will find that in the New Testament trouble is not a punishment but an opportunity. When the disciples brought to Jesus a man who was blind from birth, they asked him "Rabbi, who sinned, this man or his parents, that he was born blind?" (John 9:2). They showed their Old Testament upbringing, which always looked upon adversity as punishment for sin. And Jesus turned their thoughts in another direction. "It was not that this man sinned, or his parents, but that the works of God might be made manifest."

In other words, trouble is an opportunity, a chance to build a life after the pattern of God's Son who was "made perfect through suffering." The Apostle had his thorn in the flesh, and he prayed three times, he says, that it might be taken from him. After that he lost count; but you will find qualities of sympathy and understanding in his letters which would be missing except for that thorn. "All sunshine," says the Arab proverb, "makes a desert"; and so the ground is dry and parched and nothing will grow in it. But when you accept the fact, as we put it, that "into every life a little rain must fall," you can grow certain things that sunshine by itself could never produce.

But, you say, that takes courage. How can I stand up to trouble? You ask. How can I say to it what Jacob said to his adversary: "I will not let you go, unless you bless me" (Gen. 32:26)? And that is where the word "comforted" comes in. We think it a weak word like "consoled"; but it is our weakness which has made it weak. It is a strong word. Take the last four letters and look at them: f-o-r-t. A fort is a place of strength in which you are fortified to face the enemy. And when you put the prefix "com" in front of it, that means to be made strong by being with someone who is strong. To be comforted means to be fortified by being with Another in whose presence you can say with the Apostle, "I can do all things in him who strengthens me" (Phil. 4:13).

So the first meaning which this second beatitude has for us goes something like this: There is a certain joy which comes from seeing that when the worst happens it can be turned into the best and that the courage you need will be yours.

III

Move on and notice, in the second place, that trouble can be a source of joy in our relations with other people. That is true in a double sense, and the first is what we receive.

No man is the whole of himself; he is a social animal, and the rest of him is made up of other people. You have only to stop and realize how much a part of your happiness your friends are to know what is meant. And you who have lived long enough have discovered that there is nothing like the night to bring out the stars. "It is against dark velvet," says Ralph Sockman in his poetic way, "that diamonds are displayed to show their luster." That means that it is not in sunny times but in hours of darkness that you discover the hidden riches of friendship.

If you doubt it, only get sick and go to the hospital. People you never dreamed had an interest in you will come to visit. Let your home catch fire and burn, and you will have the offer of more homes than you can possibly live in. When sudden death strikes the family circle and you are crushed in bereavement, you have to have help in meeting the many callers; and later on, when you are looking through the cards that are left, you are amazed to discover that so many thought of you and came to bring an expression of friendship. I recently went to such a home, and by the time I arrived the two front rooms were filled with friends who had come to help. Misery loves company, and misery has a right to company, and misery gets company! How often have you had someone tell you: "I didn't know how many friends I had until this trouble came." Blessed are they that mourn, for they find how many friends they have, and they find strength in friendship.

But trouble offers a second source of joy in our relation to other people. It is more blessed to give than to receive; and often trouble is the indispensable condition of being able to help.

For example, I learned long ago that when a victim of alcoholism comes to me for help the best thing I can do for him is to get him in touch with a member of Alcoholics Anonymous. I am glad to be his friend, but I am powerless to help in the place where he needs it because I have never sat where he sits. For that reason I am grateful for my friends in AA, who hold themselves always in readiness to step in. They can help because they know the power of the passion for drink and the terror of the pink elephants. Their very trouble gives them the equipment which is needed.

The year before World War I began, a man in England named Arthur Pearson went blind. Later on soldiers began coming back from the front with sight gone, and Arthur Pearson set up a hospital for the rehabilitation of blinded men.

When a soldier went to the doctor and learned his fate, often he was plunged into despair and the doctors were helpless. Then they would call in Arthur Pearson. He would go to the man, put his hand on his shoulder and say quietly, "Remember, old fellow, I am blind too." Often the man would snap out of it and be saved from a possible suicide. There is no way of measuring the satisfaction which Arthur Pearson found in helping those 1,700 men to a new life; but it was his blindness which gave him a key to their hearts.

When you look at your trouble through the eyes of this beatitude, you can see in your experience a rite of initiation by which you have been ordained to a high calling. "Blessed be . . . God of all comfort," says Paul, "who comforts us in all affliction, so that we may be able to comfort those who are in any affliction" (II Cor. 1:3-4). And St. Francis made this his prayer: "O Divine Master, grant that I may not so much seek to be comforted as to comfort. . . . For it is in giving that we receive."

Finally, this beatitude is a promise of joy not only in our relation with ourselves and other people, but with God as well. The word "mourn" refers not only to sorrow in personal misfortune, and a concern which cares for the misfortune of others, but to a conscience which is conscious of sin. The "mourners' bench" in churches of an earlier day was the place where the penitent waited for pardon.

Ralph Sockman points out that when the word "mourn" makes us think more of sorrow for our troubles than sorrow for our sins, we simply reflect the current religious trend toward being more concerned with the evils that befall us than with the evils which we commit. But standing, as we do, so close to the events of Passion Week which culminated on Good Friday, you simply cannot overlook that cross. It is an unforgettable picture of what evil does: it takes the best life that ever lived and does it to death. It reminds you that the same thing is going on today, in our homes and in our wider relationships, whenever self-will asserts itself over God's will. And when you take in what your self-will does to your marriage and your family and your friends, then your conscience goes to work and you begin to be concerned about what you are doing. And when the sorrow that "produces a repentance" (II Cor. 7:10) does its work, then you take your seat on the mourners' bench.

But the mourners' bench has never been a final resting place. It is simply a way station on the road to the mercy seat, the place where God's grace waits to pardon. And so this second beatitude, in its major and climactic significance, says this: "Blessed are those who are penitent for their sins, for they are strong in the joy of divine forgiveness."

3.   Blessed Are the Meek

*"Blessed are the meek, for they shall inherit the
earth."—Matthew 5:5*

In an earlier day Mark Twain declared that there
was one reference in the Bible to the British
Empire, namely: "Blessed are the meek, for they
shall inherit the earth." That was intended to be
taken as a joke, as indeed it has been. The modern
American, setting out to win the world, would
never think of meekness as the road to success.
He is heir to the Anglo-Saxon self-assertiveness
which demands a Bill of Rights, and he is a
descendant of the early pioneer whose very aggres-
siveness carried the continent before him and made
a garden out of the wilderness. He knows that if
you are going to get anywhere in this world you've
got to push your way there, and so he marks this
meekness down so low that it is written off. Even
our English cousins concur; a few years ago a
British periodical in a spirit of irony offered a

framed copy of this beatitude to any meek person
who had made good.

Yet these words come from the lips of our Lord
himself. Men called him Master, and the longer
you look at him the more you are impressed by the
fact that he knew his way around in this business
called life. He does not discount meekness; he puts
a premium upon it. He even goes so far as to make
a beatitude out of it, and a beatitude is an attitude
which makes for happiness. Maybe, after all, there
is something to this meekness. Jesus seems to think
so, and he ought to know.

I

The place to begin, of course, is to ask what
Jesus means by meekness; and no sooner have
you done that than you see what it is not. Meekness, for example, is not weakness. It is so easy
to mistake one of the signs of a thing for the
thing itself. A star gives light, and so does a glowworm, but a glowworm is not a star. Meekness
is not weakness.

When you begin to look into the word, you
find that it has a history; and that history takes you
back among the Greeks. The ideal of the Greek
was the golden mean; that is, every virtue was the
mean between two extremes. So Aristotle describes

meekness as the golden mean between extreme anger and extreme angerlessness. The meek man is not the man who never knows anger; rather, he is the man who is always angry at the right time and never angry at the wrong time. When you ask what is the right time and the wrong time to be angry, you can find your answer in the experience of Jesus. He was never angry at any injury done to himself, but he did show anger at injuries or injustice to other people. The Gospel of Mark makes that plain. When he was in the synagogue ready to heal the man with the withered hand and the Pharisees looked on, ready to accuse him if he performed that work of mercy on the sabbath day: "He looked around at them with anger" (Mark 3:5). It was the same thing which you have in Paul: "Who is offended," asks the Apostle, "and I burn not?" (II Cor. 11:29 KJV). Meekness is not inconsistent with anger which is angry at the right time.

But the Greeks had a second meaning for the word "meek": it was the regular word for a wild animal which had been tamed. As a boy I used to spend the summers on my uncle's plantation in Mississippi. Every year he went to Texas and bought a carload of ponies to be used by the tenants on the place in working their crops. But these ponies were wild: they had grown up on the range in Texas and had never known what it was to be controlled by the hand of man. So now they had to be "broken," as we say; and their breaking provided a rodeo which a small boy delighted to see. First, they were corralled in a pen, then lassoed, and, much against their will, bridled and saddled. One of the tenants was an excellent rider. He mounted the pony, and you never saw such bucking in your life. But old Wash held his mount; and after several rides around the lot, the pony would come back as meek as a lamb. He had been tamed, was under control, and was ready for his owner to put him to work.

That is what meekness means: a will that has been tamed and is under control. Moses is described in the Bible as the meekest among men, and yet Moses was a man of such fiery passion that he slew an Egyptian in his youth in a fit of anger. Then Moses took himself in hand by putting himself in God's hand. Through long discipline he achieved what Michelangelo depicts in his famous statue of Moses, in the Church of San Pietro in Vincoli at Rome, where you see the marvelous repose concealing the thunder of Sinai. In practical life you get a picture of it in the little fellow who was chiding a certain big man for losing his temper. "Man," said the big fellow, "I control more temper in five minutes than you will ever know in a lifetime." Meekness is the taming of the wild animal in us so that we can be controlled and put to work in God's kingdom.

There is a third meaning of meek, and it has to do with that humility which banishes all pride. It is first cousin to our word "poor" in the first beatitude, and suggests a poverty of ego which is an emptying of self before God. It is the submission of the creature to the Creator and a feeling of dependence upon a higher power. No teacher can teach a student who knows it all already, and not even God can do anything for a man who has no sense of need.

From that angle, meekness turns out to be not weakness but strength. It was said of a certain person: He seemed a man whose will was as weak as water, but in the grip of One who made him as strong as iron. It is said also that if you place a straw parallel with the Gulf Stream, the Gulf Stream will flow through the straw. Meekness is a man placing his will in line with the will of God and saying "O God, flow through me and make me strong." It is Moses the meek standing before Pharaoh the king and saying "Let my people go." It is Jesus before Pilate, saying with his silence "Stop me if you can." It is Peter and John, laughing in the face of Jerusalem police, saying "We must obey God rather than man." It is Martin

Luther, defying the pope and saying to his princes "Here I stand." It is the namesake of that same monk, standing up to the power structure of his day and saying "We shall overcome." It is John Knox in Scotland pounding his pulpit in St. Giles, and putting Mary Stuart the queen in her place. It is any man, every man, who so fears the face of God that he is not afraid of human flesh. That is what meekness is. It is not weakness; it is strength.

II

Yet once you have put your finger on what Jesus meant by the meek man, your trouble has just begun. You have then, in the second place, to square that with what he said about meekness being the road to inheriting the earth. You will notice that he did not say "heaven." Had he said that, our task would be simpler. Then he would have been talking above our heads, out of our reach, away from our range of experience. But he doesn't say heaven; he says "the earth." The man who lets go his own way to let God have his way, who accepts life and what it brings—how in the world is he going to inherit the earth? That quality does not seem to stand out in the lives of the go-getters you know, who win sales contests and hold positions and possessions and power.

The only way I know to answer the question is to set it up against the facts as we know them in the world as it is. Is it not a matter of history that it has always been the men with the gift of self-control, the men with their impulses under discipline, who come out on top? From the job of office manager in your business to the rulers of the earth, this is a fact of life: No man can be in control of others who is not in control of himself. Even in the game of golf the great Bobby Jones said he never could become a winner until he had learned to control his temper.

Thomas Carlyle says that the lesson of life is to learn to believe what the years and the centuries say against the hours. In the light of the centuries, look at a man like Napoleon. You would never think of calling Napoleon a meek man. He was an apostle of power who sought to force his will on the world. He believed, as he put it, that God was always on the side of the biggest battalions. Yet when the Little Colonel stopped talking long enough to think, he started singing another tune. This is the way he put it: "Alexander, Caesar, Charlemagne, and myself have founded empires. But upon what did we rest the creation of our genius? Upon force, and they have crumbled into dust. Jesus Christ alone founded his empire upon love, and at this moment millions of men would die for him."

At first there were only twelve, but today that round dozen has been multiplied to six hundred million. "I am meek and lowly in heart," said Jesus (Matt. 11:29 KJV); and it does appear that "the meek shall inherit the earth."

III

So much for what it means to be meek and to inherit the earth. There is yet the word "blessed" which means happy. Wherein is the happiness which belongs to the meek? It comes from three directions, and the first is the world of things.

I like the way Lyman Abbott puts it. "Have you not met the grasping man on a journey?" he asks. "On the arrival of the train at the station he makes his way to the front, careless of the women and children whom he pushes to one side; he gets the first seat in the hotel omnibus, or is the first to drive away in a cab from the station; he succeeds in putting himself at the head of the waiting line at the hotel desk, not infrequently crowding himself in before the meeker and less assertive men; he demands the best room in the hotel and often gets it. 'Verily, verily, I say unto you, they have their reward.' But I have noticed," Mr. Abbott goes on, "that this man never enjoys his journey. He is a chronic grumbler. He finds no pleasure and he finds a multitude of faults. He may possess the earth and he often does, but he never inherits it. He gets, but he does not gain."

That picture is a parable of the larger experience which we call the journey of life. The go-getter often gets, but he rarely enjoys. I read recently about a man of wealth who said that he had spent half his life in an office making his money and the other half in the courts trying to keep other people from taking it away from him. So absorbed was he in these endeavors that he had no time left for the cultivation of appreciation and enjoyment.

But meekness makes for happiness not only in your relation to the things of the world but in your relation to other people, and that in two ways.

First, because it makes so many friends. It is fascinating to discover what the French make out of the key word in this text. When they translated their New Testament, what they put here is this: "Blessed are the debonair." You know what debonair means: it means affable, courteous, gentlemanly—literally, of good mien. Someone defines a gentleman as one who refuses to put his own rights before the feelings of others. That is the essence of the genius of friendship. In the

43

alphabet of charm, we are told, there is no such thing as the letter "I"; it is all "U." That is what meekness is: It is getting the I, the ego, out of the way. And it is the people who can do that, the affable, the courteous, the debonair, who know the joy of friendship.

Furthermore, meekness makes for happiness with other people because it does not get angry at wrongs done against self and is free from grudges. The late William Anderson, minister of a church in Dallas, once told me this story. A lady he had never seen before came to his study one day. "Doctor," she said, "I haven't got any peace in my heart, and I came to see if you can help me find it." He asked if she had a guilty conscience for any known sin, and she said she hadn't. He asked if she hated anybody, and she said she didn't. Then he suggested that they call God into the conference. They bowed their heads, and Dr. Anderson began to pray. "O God," he prayed, "this woman says she wants peace in her heart. She says she is not guilty of any sin. She says she does not hate anybody; I don't believe her, but, God, you know better than I do." And with that the woman said out loud, "I don't hate her any more." Dr. Anderson closed his prayer and then asked her, "You don't hate whom any more?" "My mother-in-law," she answered. And then it all came out, her grudge against her mother-in-law which had made a grave for her happiness. Dr. Anderson led her penitence into confession, and she found forgiveness and, finally, the peace which she sought.

There is no heart on this earth big enough to hold hatred and happiness within itself. "It burns me up," you say; and it does. But the meek man keeps himself free from hatred because he puts his ego out of the way and never lets it get angry at personal wrongs. Blessed are the meek, for they shall inherit a happiness free from grudges.

Finally, the meek man inherits happiness not only in relation to the things of this earth and the people of this earth, but also in relation to the God of this earth.

Here we come to the essence of meekness. It is letting go your own way and letting God have his way. It is taking life out of your own hands and putting it into God's hands, and saying to him, "O God, do with me and make of me what thou wilt." When Thomas Carlyle was told that a certain woman had said "I accept the universe," he replied "Egad, she'd better!" And so had we.

You see, this world was here before you came along. It has its own constitution and laws, its own conditions under which life must be lived. You have no right to demand that God make it over to suit your taste, as you might ask a landlord to do over an apartment to fit your desires. If you seek to impose your will upon life, you will resent any interference with your plans; and then when you go broke or go blind and everything goes berserk, your castle in the sand will be dashed to pieces by one little wave of misfortune.

How much better to see that this world is bigger than you are, and has within it a purpose larger than your private wishes. It is a purpose in which all things can be made to work together for good, and behind which is a Person whose name is love and whose resources are at your disposal. To accept that purpose and that Person, so that you put his will above your wish, is the very heart of meekness and the very key to happiness.

The founder of the Salvation Army was William Booth of England. Late in life he lost his sight, and his son Bramwell was sent to break the news to him that he would never see again. "You mean that I am blind," said the general. "I fear that we must contemplate that," his son answered. "I shall never see your face again?" asked the general. "No," said Bramwell, "probably not." The old man's hand moved across the bedcovers until it held his son's. "Bramwell," he said, "I have done what I could for God and the people with my

46

eyes. Now I shall do what I can for God and the people without my eyes."

Resentment? No. Bitterness? No. Acceptance? Yes! And with it the general was the same blithe spirit he had always been.

4. Blessed Are Those Who Hunger and Thirst

"Blessed are those who hunger and thirst for righteousness, for they shall be satisfied."
—*Matthew 5:6*

Someone has described a small boy as "an appetite with a skin drawn over it," and we know how true that is. Yet the small boy, had he a mind to do so, might turn the definition back upon the rest of us and ask "Why single me out?" For all of life—everyone's life—is appetite in search of gratification. We are creatures of desire, each of us, all the way from appetite for something to eat up to a craving to know God better.

That is all very well, for the secret of happiness is desire, plus that which satisfies desire. A healthy appetite is the first condition of an enjoyable meal; while if there be no appetite, the sight of food can easily become nauseating. The desire for knowledge can make education one long and glorious holiday; while if there be no desire, life can become the world's worst abomination. The love of another can make a heaven out of earth; while if there be no interest in the person who proffers it, there is nothing more repellent. Desire plays its essential role in all happiness, and Jesus was right: Blessed are those who hunger and thirst.

But there are those who think that Jesus went on and threw cold water over everything. He is correct in linking happiness with desire and its gratification, but he does not list the usual objects of desire. What he says is this: "Blessed are those who hunger and thirst for righteousness." That is a horse of another color, and so we must begin by asking what he meant.

I

Take first of all his word "righteousness." This is an old and, to some people, an ugly and forbidding word. There are those who would try to bundle up the demands of righteousness in a little set of rules, saying "Thou shalt not do this" and "Thou shalt not do that"—thinking that when such petty requirements have been met, the matter is settled. It was so with the Pharisee. The conventional standard of righteousness had to do with such things as keeping the sabbath and tithing and fasting so many times a week; and the Pharisee felt that when he had obeyed the rules he was one hundred percent right, so he became self-righteous. But self-righteousness is a long sea mile from what Jesus had in mind.

In a word, righteousness is rightness: rightness as measured by a correct standard. Whenever you want to know whether your foot rule measures twelve inches, or your bushel basket holds four pecks, or your scales are showing sixteen ounces to the pound, you can test them by the standard. The government maintains in Washington a Bureau of Standard Weights and Measures, and you can see how they square with the standard.

Now in the matter of righteousness there is a standard also, and that standard is the character of God as portrayed in his Son. If you wish to know whether or not you are righteous, just walk up to Jesus Christ and stand beside him and see how you square with such a character! He does not say "Keep the Ten Commandments and you will be righteous." He says "Love God with all of you and your neighbor as yourself." He says "A new commandment give I to you, that you love one another; even as I have loved you" (John 13:34). He says "You, therefore, must be perfect, as your heavenly Father is perfect" (Matt. 5:48).

When you begin to take in the meaning of the

demands of righteousness, which is a life which squares with the divine character as revealed in Jesus Christ, you are overwhelmed. Why, you say, I am not a god; I am a son of Adam, marred by all the flaws in this human clay. Who does Jesus think I am, making my happiness depend upon a goal so far out of my reach? And then, when you arrive at that point, you are ready to take in what Jesus actually said. He does not mock a man by offering a reward for something he knows you will never attain. He does not say, mind you, "Blessed are the righteous," but "Blessed are those who hunger and thirst for righteousness." He does not make the possession of righteousness the condition of blessedness, but only the desire.

II

Yet the desire for Godlikeness must be all-consuming. It is not enough that it be a fleeting fancy, an occasional wish. It must be so constant and compelling that it becomes a passion. Notice that it is a desire to which Jesus likens the strongest craving—things like hunger and thirst.

William Barclay reminds us that words do not exist in isolation, but their meaning is conditioned by the background of those who speak and those to whom they are spoken. In our affluent society

it is utterly impossible for us to take in the intensity
of desire which is meant by hunger and thirst. But
in Palestine in the time of Jesus it was different.
A working man was never far from the border
line of real hunger and actual starvation, and water
cisterns were a matter of life and death. The
hunger of this beatitude is not the kind which can
be satisfied by a midmorning snack, and the thirst
is not such as can be slaked by a coffee break. It
is the hunger of a man who is starving for food,
and the thirst of a man who will die unless he
drinks.

There is a story of a young man who went to
Gautama Buddha and asked to be shown the path
of true deliverance, and Buddha led him down to
the river. It was bathing time, and the seeker assumed he was to undergo the rite of purification.
When they were some distance out in the stream,
Buddha suddenly grabbed the man and pushed his
head under water, and held it there. Finally, in
a last gasp, the fellow wrenched himself loose and
his head came up. Quietly Buddha asked him:
"When you thought you were drowning, what did
you desire most?" "Air," said the man. And Buddha
replied, "When you want salvation as much as you
wanted air, then you will get it."

The great Augustine once prayed "O God, make
me pure, but not now." Such a lukewarm wish for

goodness has no place in this beatitude. Like the
starving man who craves food and drink and the
drowning man who gasps for air is he who
hungers and thirsts for righteousness.

III

So much for the words "hunger" and "thirst" and
the word "righteousness." There is still the word
with which the beatitude begins, and that word
is "blessed." How is it that a strong desire for life
that is like God's life can bring happiness? The
answer is not far to see.

For one thing, it accords well with the facts of
our experience to say that happiness is utterly
dependent upon a unified self. Years ago I read a
sentence which has stayed with me word for word,
no doubt because it says something which is so
real. "Happiness," writes William H. Sheldon, "is
essentially a state of going somewhere whole-
heartedly, one-directionally, without regret or
reservation." That is, it comes from a unified self,
and you know how often that unity is shattered.

E. Stanley Jones says that one day his little girl
was told by her mother to do a certain thing. "I
don't want to," she replied. "All right," said her
mother, "do the other thing." "I don't want to,"
said the child. The mother, her mind preoccupied

with other duties said, "All right, so do what you want to do." And the little girl, miserable in her divided mind, said, "I don't want to do what I want to do."

That comes close enough home for all of us to know how that little girl felt. She did not know her own mind, as we say. She was like a man betting on two horses, not knowing which he wanted to win. She was like a football team without a quarterback, like an army without a general, like sheep without a shepherd. She was like a broom, ending in a multitude of small straws, instead of like a sword, in point and power; and her mind was like a brush heap, a miscellaneous pile of twigs and branches instead of like a tree, a vital and growing entity.

When you set out on your search for happiness, you discover how fatal to the quest is the divided mind. Jesus said once that a house divided against itself cannot stand; and he might have gone on and said that a man divided against himself cannot stand—himself! In a recent cartoon a physician faces his patient in anxious solemnity, saying: "This is a very serious case: I'm afraid you're allergic to yourself." When you face this disunity within yourself, and are honest enough to see and to say that you don't want to do what you want to do, you are indeed allergic to yourself; and as long as you remain so, happiness is only a dream well out of reach.

The students of human nature have only one thing to say to you: Get organized! The trouble with you is not that you're a man; you're a mob. You are a civil war. The basic desires within you have chosen sides and are in a tug-of-war. You are in the middle of a traffc jam—and I have never yet seen a man in a traffic jam who was happy about it. The only way out of a traffic jam is to bring in an officer of the law who can give an order and get it obeyed; and the only way out of a divided self is to call in some one desire and give it authority over all the rest. Only so can you find rest from yourself and find the happiness you seek.

And it is just that which Jesus does in this beatitude. He sets up a dominant desire. He offers a major motive. He presents a preeminent passion. He says "Blessed are those who hunger and thirst after a likeness to God more than they desire anything else, for they shall find happiness which belongs only to the man whose civil war has ended in peace and who no longer does not want to do what he wants to do."

One day a young man went to see Harry Emerson Fosdick and said this to him: "I want to get organized. I shall never be happy until I am organized." If you can see yourself in that young man, then this fourth beatitude has a word for you: "Blessed are those who hunger and thirst for righteousness, for in this dominant desire your life will be organized, and you will find the happiness which comes from a unified self."

IV

Go on and note, furthermore, that this hunger for the highest makes for happiness because it alone can achieve its desire in the face of all the facts of experience.

The things which people desire supremely are not many in number. They can be listed on the fingers of one hand. The first is pleasure: Long ago a teacher named Epicurus decided that pleasure was the end and aim of existence, and Epicureans are with us still. The second is fame: The hunger for the headlines, the desire for a name that is writ large in the affairs of men, is what some seek most. The third is money: The desire to make a killing and get rich is the strongest drive behind some men. The fourth is power: The hunger to dominate and control and rule is what others would sell their souls to get. The fifth and last is to grow a soul, to achieve a character, to become a real person.

There is one factor common to the first four of

these five supreme desires, and that is that they are
at the mercy of the world of circumstances. If you
are out to have a good time, the world can deny
you the means and your desire is thwarted. If you
are out to win fame, the world can pass you by
and forget you and bury your name under the dust
heap of oblivion. If you are out to make money,
the world can bring on a depression or a time
of inflation and strip you clean and make you as
poor as Job's turkey. If you are out to win power,
the scepter can be snatched from your hand and,
like Napoleon, you will find yourself on your own
St. Helena, exiled to pine away without your
power. You have your desire, but the world has
robbed you of your power to fulfill it, and you are
of all men most miserable.

Yet when you hunger and thirst after righteousness, when you make the life of God as presented
in Christ the end and aim of existence, then you
are not at the mercy of the world, and nothing can
cheat you of the chance to fulfill your desire. Instead of being thwarted by the dark facts which
to others seem the denial of desire, you actually
thrive upon them. As far as I am able to make out,
this is the only desire which can take all of life
and make it grist for the mill. It does so because it
capitalizes upon liabilities and turns them into
assets. It uses trouble as an aviator uses a stiff

headwind: as something to take off against and rise higher by. Poverty can make you more sympathetic, pain can make you more understanding, the loneliness of bereavement can open the door for a new Presence. Your blessedness stands secure because you know that if the worst happens, it can be turned into the best. And you find yourself singing the words of the old spiritual: "Nobody knows the trouble I've seen, Glory, Hallelujah!"

V

Go on to note, finally, that the hunger for the highest makes for happiness because it is the one desire which never gets fed up.

One reason why happiness for some people is like the pot of gold at the end of the rainbow is that for them life has gone stale. If it has lost its taste for you and you find that you are bored stiff, check on yourself and you will discover that you have centered your desires upon objects which do not satisfy but which satiate. What satisfies gives pleasure, while what satiates produces disgust. It is like the old song which said "When you get what you want you don't want it." That feeling is so general that it has produced a philosophy which goes like this. If you fail to get what you want, you are disappointed. If you succeed in getting what you want, you are disgusted. Either way you will be unhappy: therefore, the only way out is existence without desire.

Yet we are not shut up in this blind alley; for while it is possible to be satiated without being satisfied, it is also possible to be satisfied without being satiated. It all depends upon the object of desire. "Man is an animal which alone among the animals refuses to be satisfied by the fulfillment of animal desires"—so says Bernard Iddings Bell. Once you set your affections upon things that are above, you will break the vicious circle which ends by being fed up.

Have you ever met the man who felt that he had caught up with Christ? Have you ever considered that you had arrived at the ideal set up by the man of Galilee? It is the sense of his always being out ahead of you that gives to Christ his charm. Strive as hard as you will, you will never arrive; and yet all the while your striving is arriving.

Paul sums it for us. "Brethren," he says, "I do not consider that I have made it my own; but one thing I do, forgetting what lies behind and straining forward to what lies ahead, I press on toward the goal for the prize of the upward call of God in Christ Jesus" (Phil. 3:13-14).

"I press on," he says, and find my joy in the endless pursuit of a flying goal. That is what this beatitude means, and that is the challenge which it presents: "Blessed are those who hunger and thirst for righteousness, for they shall be satisfied."

5. Blessed Are the Merciful

"Blessed are the merciful, for they shall obtain mercy."—Matthew 5:7

In the tropical forests of the East Indies is a flower which has a putrid scent when taken by itself, but which has a pleasant odor when mingled with the other scents of the forest. It is so with those qualities of human character which we call the virtues. If one is developed out of proportion to the others, it sometimes has a bad odor; and more than one writer sees a reason behind the juxtaposition of the fourth and fifth beatitudes.

Take, for example, the virtue which claimed our attention in the last chapter. The person who hungers and thirsts after righteousness in the narrow sense desires above all else to be right, but when this desire issues in self-righteousness, it is most unattractive. The desire to be right needs to be corrected by its opposite, the desire to show mercy; and so we are not surprised to discover that

after speaking of the hunger and thirst after right-
ousness Jesus begins to talk about the merciful.

And the correction works both ways. Just as
righteousness needs mercy to be kept in proportion, so does mercy need righteousness to strike a
true balance. Mercy which has at its heart no pro-
test against unrighteousness easily becomes soft
and soon becomes sentimentality. And so while
righteousness without mercy is ruthless, mercy
without righteousness is mushy. The two virtues go
together in life, and so Jesus puts them together in
his teaching.

Having set the two in proper proportion, he goes
ahead to pronounce a beatitude upon the merciful:
"Blessed are the merciful, for they shall obtain
mercy." It becomes our task now to discover how
happiness is to be had by showing mercy. The
answer lies by way of finding out what is meant
by mercy.

I

The first meaning is the most obvious one. If
you were asked what it means to be merciful,
you would answer right off the bat that it means
to show kindness to the unfortunate. It means pity
for the poor and help for the needy. It is Red Cross
work, so to speak. It means being a Good Samari-

tan, picking up the wounded and caring for the distressed. A hospital is a place of healing for the broken bodies of people, and it is no accident that in one city where I lived there was one hospital named Mercy and another named Good Samaritan. It simply suggests the initial meaning of this word, that to be merciful is to be like the Samaritan who went about doing good. It is Golden Rule Christianity.

But the kind of mercy which will fulfill the Golden Rule needs to be more than compassion for the unfortunate: it involves an imaginative understanding. If you wish to do for some other person what you would like him to do for you, then you must be able to put yourself in his place and see what life looks like through his eyes. It seems there are customs in the use of words just as there are styles in the cut of clothing, and here are two words which now are very much in style. One of these words is "empathy." I looked it up in the dictionary, and what it means is this: the capacity for participating in another's feelings or ideas. Another expression that is in style right now is to speak of "identifying with" another. That means practically the same thing. To identify with another is to be able to put yourself in his place by an act of imaginative understanding. And the capacity to show mercy requires the capacity to participate in another's feelings by putting yourself in his place.

Our city of Greensboro has had a visit from a remarkable man. He is Dr. Paul Tournier of Geneva, Switzerland, who has become widely known throughout the world by his writings. Sir William Osler used to say to his medical students, "Young gentlemen, the first requisite in the care of the patient is to care." Dr. Tournier fulfills that requirement, and it has led to his unique kind of practice which is called the "medicine of the person." Because of his Christian compassion he enters into full empathy with his patient and identifies with him completely; and as a result he sees it as his business not so much to treat the disease which a patient has as to treat the patient who has the disease. When you listen to him talk and read his books, you have the feeling that with him a patient is not just another case but a person. The healing ministry is a ministry of mercy par excellence, and in the hands of Dr. Tournier it is more than compassion: it is imaginative understanding.

When you set out to incarnate this beatitude, you can learn the art of showing mercy from the Master who spoke it. He imaginatively saw the Prodigal's problem from within. He became blind

Bartimaeus when the cry rose from the roadside. He saw from within the way life looked to Zacchaeus, and from within he knew the secret sifting of Peter's soul by Satan. He saw men as one sees stained glass in a cathedral window: not from without in, but from within out. And when you are moved to show mercy to another—whether to a friend who has lost a loved one, or to a child in his schoolwork, or to the Negro in his need— you will want to possess not only a feeling of compassion but an imaginative understanding which is willing to identify with him.

And Jesus says that such kindness will make for happiness. "Blessed are the merciful, for they shall obtain mercy." He does not mean that if you care for the needy, then others will care for you. At least it did not work out that way for him. Some incurable optimist has put it that if you cast your bread upon the waters it will come back to you buttered; but I shall never forget one disillusioned man who told me that if you cast it forth it might come back, but when it does it will be wet and soggy and no good for eating.

Yet Jesus is correct: when you go out of your way to show kindness to another, you will find an open door to happiness for this reason, that most unhappiness comes from self-centeredness.

One young woman wrote this note to explain her suicide: "I am taking my life because I have never sincerely loved any human being in all my life." If you begin by centering yourself on yourself, you will end by not liking the self you are centered on. But the moment you move self out to the circumference and put someone else at the center, you will find that the reflex of kindness is happiness.

"He who loses his life shall find it." (Matt. 10:39.) Jesus said that a long time ago, but the doctors are just beginning to learn the wisdom of prescribing it. For example, Karl Menninger is one of the founders of the Menninger Psychiatric Clinic in Kansas. He was asked by a newspaper reporter: "Suppose that you suspect you're heading for a nervous breakdown. What would you do?" You'd have thought that a great psychiatrist would have said "Go to see a psychiatrist." But this is what he did say: "Go straight to your front door, turn the knob, cross the tracks, and find somebody who needs you."

One of our friends told us that the only way she found a way out of the anguish of bereavement was to offer her friendship to another in her need. Jesus is right: "Blessed are the merciful, for they shall obtain mercy."

II

But to say that mercy means kindness to the needy is simply to say the obvious, and the deeper meanings of the beatitude are never obvious. They do not lie on the surface, and you have to dig down to get them. When you take your mental spade and begin the business of excavation, you will find that Jesus is defining here your attitude to the morally as well as the physically unfit. Mercy means not only kindness to the unfortunate but grace to the guilty. It is the Good Samaritan helping the poor traveler, but it is more. It is Jesus on the cross, praying for those who put him there. with a prayer for forgiveness.

I suppose one of the commonest experiences people have is to be hurt by someone else. An unkind word, a stab in the back, a tricky deal by which some member of the family cheats you out of your share in the inheritance: in any one of a number of ways you are nailed to the cross as was Jesus. You have a problem on your hands, and in one way or another you must deal with that situation.

Human nature being what it is, your first desire is for revenge. You would know what Heine meant when he wrote, only half in jest: "My wishes are a humble dwelling with a thatched roof, a good bed, good food, flowers at my window, and some fine tall trees before my door. And if the good God wants to make me completely happy, he will grant me the joy of seeing six or seven of my enemies hanging from the trees." Michelangelo was a genius in many ways, but he proved himself small in his vindictiveness; for when the pope's master of ceremonies criticized one of his figures, the artist painted a portrait of his critic and put it in his picture of hell, and there left him to be a laughingstock of Rome.

But of course you are supposed to be a Christian, and a Christian is supposed to love his enemies; and so with a glow of self-approval you tell yourself that you will forgive. But you make it clear that while you will forgive, you can never forget. What you have done is to forgo the desire for revenge, but you continue to harbor resentment.

The more you study the mind of Christ, the more you see the emphasis he placed upon two emotional attitudes as the enemies of human welfare. One is fear and the other is hatred, and the reason he was out to get them both was that he knew how destructive both are to human health and happiness. Allow your mind to be filled with either anxiety or anger, and you sign over all rights to happiness and eventually to health.

Harry Emerson Fosdick tells about a woman

who came to him for counsel. She hated her sister, she said. Her sister did not know it; nobody knew it. But years before, her sister, with perfectly good intentions, had prevented this woman's marriage; and ever since that time a smoldering resentment had set in. Outwardly she was cordial and friendly toward her sister but inwardly she harbored a grudge, and now she was on the verge of collapse. She was a nervous wreck, gone to pieces, both health and happiness torn to shreds. And Dr. Fosdick, in pointing out her difficulty, used a sentence I have never forgotten: "Hating somebody is like burning down your house to get rid of a rat."

When once you see that revenge and resentment are the way to unhappiness, then you are readier to listen to this beatitude and to try the way of mercy which forgives wrongs done against it and refuses to take account of snubs and slights and evils. Simon Peter came to Jesus and said "How often shall I forgive a man, seven times?" And Jesus answered: "Not seven times, not even seven times seven times, but seventy times seven times." Seventy times seven is 490; and the idea is that there is no limit. Your feeling is that it is perfectly fine for the person forgiven but utterly unjust to the other. But sooner or later you come to see that mercy which forgives is not a luxury in human relations; it is a necessity for all who would know happiness.

III

There is yet a higher rung on the ladder of blessedness waiting for the merciful. Not only does it save him from himself by centering his interest outside himself; not only does it oil the machinery and keep him from a crack-up in the world of human relationships; but mercy is also the key which unlocks the door into the presence of God. It is the ticket to the Eternal, and to the blessedness of living in that fellowship.

That is what Jesus means when he says the merciful shall obtain mercy. It is not a mere tit-for-tat. It does not mean that because you are willing to forgive a person who has wronged you, therefore God is willing to return the favor and forgive you. To obtain mercy is not to be paid back in kind for mercy which you have shown. It is something far more fundamental. It is described not as the grounds but as the condition for obtaining mercy.

It is simply the working out of a principle in our relationship with God which holds true throughout all life, the principle that like can be known only by like. In the parable of the unmerciful servant a man was forgiven a debt and immediately refused to forgive a debtor; whereupon his master was wroth and delivered him to his tormentors. Then Jesus added: "So also my heavenly Father will do to every one of you, if you do not forgive your brother from your heart" (Matt. 18:35). Jesus never bribed men to be good: he is not hiring them to be merciful with offers of mercy. He is simply saying that you cannot marry the merciful and the unmerciful, and showing that a man shuts himself out from the presence of God when he fails to show mercy.

John Wesley used the same argument with Governor Oglethorpe of the Georgia colony. It happened that a servant had broken open and drunk several bottles of the governor's rare wine. Wesley interceded for the offender and tried to calm the enraged Oglethorpe. "Sir," shouted the irate governor, "I never forgive." "Then," replied Wesley, "I hope you never offend." You cannot mix oil and water. Like can be known only by like. So the merciful shall obtain mercy, because only so can man know and be restored to fellowship with the God whose name is mercy.

More than once I have had someone come to my study with this question: How can I learn to forgive another who has wronged me? I knew the problem was a real one, and I believe that in each case the desire to forgive was honest; but it is never easy.

The only answer I knew was to tell a story about a communion service in a Methodist church in New Zealand, where some of those present had only recently come out of barbarism into Christianity. One man went forward and knelt at the communion rail, then returned to his seat without receiving the elements. A few minutes later he returned to the rail and knelt, and this time took communion. When asked the reason for his unusual behavior, he said this: "The first time I went forward I found myself kneeling next to the man who had murdered my father and against whom I had sworn vengeance. I was full of hate, and I could not take communion. So I went back to my seat; but as I sat there, I seemed to see three crosses. On the center cross was a man who was praying, and he was saying 'Father, forgive them, for they know not what they do.' Then I could not stay away, and so I went back and took communion next to the man who had been my enemy."

That is what it means to obtain mercy. It is to be restored to communion with God; and when you find that fellowship, you will find also the blessedness which is the promise of this beatitude.

6.   Blessed Are the Pure in Heart

"Blessed are the pure in heart, for they shall see God."—Matthew 5:8

When the poet Tennyson was well along in years, he asked his son, who was to be the executor of his estate, to see that the publishers, when they collected his poems and put them in a single volume, placed "Crossing the Bar" at the end of the book. No reason was given for such a request; but perhaps there is a clue in the fact that when Tennyson was asked once what was his dearest wish, he answered, "A clearer vision of God." It would therefore seem an appropriate climax that the book should end with those lines which speak of seeing his Pilot "face to face" when he had "crossed the bar."

This vision of God, which was the poet's wish, is the theme of the sixth beatitude: "Blessed are the pure in heart," said Jesus, "for they shall see God." As we seek to make our way into the

Master's meaning, it will be helpful to begin at the end of the line and work toward the front.

I

That brings us first then to the words which speak of seeing God, and it is natural to wonder what he meant by that. You remember that John put it down in black and white that "No one has ever seen God" (John 1:18); and yet here Jesus is making a promise as clearly as words can say it that men shall see God. What can he mean by that?

I am sure that there must be a clue in the verb which Jesus uses. He speaks of seeing God, and it is no mere coincidence that among your five physical senses the most dominant is the sense of sight. That has been proved over and over again. In a certain English school a class of boys was sent into a room for two minutes and then brought back to write out a list of things noticed while there. The lists varied in length from ten to forty objects, but the most significant part of the experiment was that nothing was listed except things that had been seen. In that room were the noises which came in from the street, the sound of a piano in another part of the building, and the scent of a cigar which had been purposely introduced; and yet not one of these was mentioned by the students.

It is because of experiments like this that our students of human nature are telling us that the things we see make a deeper impression on us than the things which we hear or touch or taste or smell. It is a fact, proved by experiment and experience, that while you remember only two-fifths of what you hear, you remember three-fifths of what you see, and four-fifths of what you both see and hear. You can understand the reason then for the immense influence of television and movies on the minds of children. It is because they reach the city of Mansoul through the Eyegate. Long years ago the Chinese discovered what we are talking about and wrapped the truth up in one of their proverbs: "One picture," they said, "is worth more than ten thousand words." Why? Because what you see gets hold of you, and sight is the sense which makes something most real to you.

Yet if you are going to understand what Jesus means, you have to recognize the fact that there are several kinds of seeing. There is, first of all, physical sight. When you go to your doctor to learn whether or not you need to change your glasses, he puts a card in front of you with letters of several sizes and asks if you can see them. That is physical sight. Then, secondly, there is mental vision, by which through the eye of the mind you can see and understand truth. You say, I see your reasons, I see that two and two make four; I see why it has to be so. Then, again, there is spiritual vision, by which through the eyes of the soul you can go beyond discerning a material object, or understanding an abstract truth, to apprehending a spiritual presence. When you shut your eyes, you can still see—you can see him who is invisible.

A group of students in a midwestern college was meeting for a forum during spiritual emphasis week, and the question of God came up. "How many in this room believe in God?" the leader asked. Every hand went straight up. Then he asked this question: "To how many in this room is God real?" Scarcely one hesitant hand was raised.

That brings us closer to the thinking of Jesus. When he speaks of seeing God, he does not mean that you see him in the sense that you can see the person sitting next to you in the pew; he means rather that you can know him as a presence that is real. Just as by the sense of sight you can best grasp the reality of anything, so to speak of seeing God is to emphasize the certainty of your ability to know him in experience.

Before the days of television, people used to entertain themselves in more personal ways. I

76

have always liked the story of the English hostess who had among her guests a well-known actor of the day and asked him to recite the twenty-third psalm for the group. He consented, and with perfect diction, a well-modulated voice, and proper intonations he gave a polished reading, and was rewarded with warm applause. For some reason another member of the group, an unpretentious man unknown outside the circle of his closest friends, was requested to follow suit with the same subject, and he modestly agreed. There was nothing of the practiced art of the public speaker but only the eloquence which comes from being in dead earnest. The audience was deeply moved, and when he finished everybody was silent. The same question was in the minds of all present: why the difference in effect between the two. The first speaker understood and was gracious enough to admit it: "I know the psalm," he explained, "but he knows the Shepherd."

Many of you are acquainted with a German theologian named Dietrich Bonhoeffer who was put to death in a concentration camp. On the twentieth anniversary of Bonhoeffer's execution there was an article about him in a magazine, and one of his fellow prisoners who knew him best had this to say about him: "He was one of the very few men that I have ever met to whom his

God was real and close to him" (Payne Best of Britain).

I take it that that is what Jesus means by "seeing God."

II

So much for the *what* of the text. Move back toward the front and you will notice that Jesus goes on to speak of the *how*. "Blessed are the pure in heart, for they shall see God," he says.

There is a principle which runs throughout life and says that what you see depends in large measure upon what you see with. You find it even in our nursery rhymes.

> Pussycat, pussycat, where have you been?
> "I've been to London to visit the queen."
> Pussycat, pussycat, what did you there?
> "I frightened a little mouse under a chair."

What you see depends upon what you see with, and a cat's eyes would not be cats' eyes if they looked at the queen and forgot the mouse.

It is a principle written also in human life. A party of tourists was being conducted through a European art gallery. When it was over, the guide said, "And now, ladies and gentlemen, if you

have any questions, I shall be happy to answer."
One lady spoke up: "I wish you would tell me
what brand of polish is used to keep these floors
so shiny." An artist and a timber merchant stood
watching a sunset paint the landscape golden.
"It is glorious, isn't it?" said the artist. "Yes," said
the merchant. "I figure that, allowing for cutting
and hauling, it ought to work out to about eighty
cents a foot." Time and again I have heard someone say concerning a friend: "I have never been
able to understand why she married that man. For
the life of me, I can't see what she sees in him."
What you see in this world depends upon what
you see with, and these individual differences in
sight equipment do not eliminate but illustrate
our truth.

It is the "pure in heart," says Jesus, who "see
God." What does he mean by that? The answer
is a double one.

The word "pure" in the New Testament occurs
twenty-eight times, and ten times it is translated
"clean." The picture is that of soiled linen that is
washed clean of dirt, and that suggests the first
idea. God is purity itself, and it is a fact of
life that purity and dirt do not mix. If you fill
your mind with dirty thoughts, there is no room
left for God. If you spend your time reading dirty
books and telling dirty stories, you shut the door

in his face. If you delight in dirty movies, there is little wonder God is a stranger to you. What you see depends upon what you see with. Only the pure in heart see God, and when your lenses are smeared with dirt your vision is blurred.

That is the meaning which you usually give to these words, and yet there is a deeper significance which is dominant. The word "heart" in the Bible usually means the whole personality, and it includes the mind and the will along with the emotions. It means not only clean, in the sense that it is free from dirt, but it also means unmixed, in the sense of singleness of motive. It means linen that is washed clean, and it means also gold that is unalloyed. We use the word in the same way. We speak of our pure food laws: of sugar that is pure sugar, of milk that is pure milk, of soap that is 99 and 44/100 percent pure. We mean something that is unmixed, unalloyed with any foreign element. Jesus made it clear that the publicans and the harlots would go into the kingdom sooner than the self-righteous, not because they were like Ivory Soap, but because they were sincere; because they were single-minded, because their motives were unmixed.

I have a minister friend with a sense of humor who, with his tongue in his cheek, has a way of speaking of his physical eye and his spiritual eye.

But if he really meant that—if he were really like a man betting on two horses and not knowing which he wanted to win, with his loyalty divided half-and-half between the things of this world and the things of the spirit—he would never see God. You simply cannot reach the promised land of God's presence if, all the while you are marching through the wilderness of this life, you are casting wistful glances in the direction of Egypt, sniffing for a scent of garlic, and wishing for the pleasures of sin for a season. To try to stand with one foot in the church and the other right in the middle of some unethical business deal or immoral personal relationship—to try to hold on to God with one hand, and with the other to make friends with the devil—is to give up any chance at the promise of this beatitude. "If therefore thine eye be single," says Jesus, "thy whole body shall be full of light" (Matt. 6:22 KJV); but trying to look in two directions at once, splitting your loyalty in half, giving only a part to God and holding part for yourself is to live in darkness and to lose the sense of the divine presence.

Ralph W. Sockman has a way of putting our truth which makes it more easily remembered. He notes the frequent use of the word "walk" in the New Testament: "Walk in love," "Walk in the light," "Walk in newness of life." And then he says this: "We enter into truth feet first even more than head first." And that is biblical doctrine. When the scribes questioned the authority of Jesus to teach and asked how he could know when he had never even been to school he answered them like this: "If any man's will is to do his will, he shall know" (John 7:17). And Robertson of Brighton, that British preacher who is still read and quoted after more than a hundred years, took that verse and delivered a sermon on it which he called "Obedience, the Organ of Spiritual Knowledge."

So then, if you wish to see God, if you want to know his presence as something that is real, find out what he wants you to do and make up your mind that you are going to do it, whole-heartedly, single-mindedly, without *if* or *but.* That is what it means to be pure in heart, and that is the open door to the vision of God.

III

Notice, finally, that Jesus pronounces a beatitude upon this experience. Because the pure in heart see God, therefore they are blessed. That vision is the Beatific Vision. When you put all your eggs in one basket and gamble on God, then you will see him, you will know the meaning of blessedness. Why and how can that fact be true?

A man named G. A. Johnston Ross was a professor in the Union Theological Seminary in New York. He was a teacher of preachers, and one of his fellow professors writes that he was always telling the students that the primary purpose of every sermon, as well as of the worship service, was to make men aware of God, for if they could know the divine presence, most of their problems would look different in that light. If in some way this chapter could lead you to see God in the sense that he becomes as real to you as a member of your family, then yours would be the blessedness which comes from solving the things which make you unhappy.

The misery of a divided mind is gone because God unites the heart. The wretchedness of worry is gone because you can let him do your worrying for you. The bitterness of anger and envy and jealousy is gone because it is washed away by something called love. The hell of a guilty conscience is gone because the slate is wiped clean with his word of gracious pardon. The burden of boredom is gone because the will of God is like a thread which strings the purposeless days into a necklace of meaning. Sir Walter Scott said once: "When I married my wife before the altar, there and then there entered my heart the peace which passeth understanding." It is the peace of a presence—the presence of a friend named God; when you have that presence, you have that peace; and when you have that peace, you have found your blessedness.

When the last war came on, the government passed a draft law and began sending out questionnaires to prospective draftees. A questionnaire is always Greek to me, and I have full sympathy with that unlettered man in our Southland who received one. He got the point of it, and without going into detailed answers to all the questions, he wrote this message across the face of the thing: "Dear Uncle Sam: Your letter has come, and I just want you to know I'm ready when you're ready," signed it and sent it in.

That is what it means to be pure in heart: To be pure in heart is to see God, and to see God is to know the meaning of true blessedness.

7. Blessed Are the Peacemakers

"Blessed are the peacemakers, for they shall be called sons of God."—Matthew 5:9

Albert W. Beaven used to say that there is one word which sums up our contemporary life and that word is "split." In ourselves we are often split personalities. In our homes our families are frequently split. In our country we are split between capital and labor, between white and black. In our world we are split between East and West, and now these two monolithic power blocs are developing crevices which are becoming ever more apparent. It does seem that the word "split" has meaning wherever you look.

Some years ago a Jewish rabbi named Joshua Liebman wrote a best-selling book called *Peace of Mind.* He began it with the statement that in his youth he made a list of things to be desired: health and wealth and talent and power and fame and a few others. Showing his list to a wise older

85

friend, he was told that he had left out one ingredient without which every other possession would be meaningless. That one thing is peace of mind; and along with peace of mind, there go peace in the home, and peace in the land, and world peace.

In the beatitudes Jesus is telling us that true happiness depends more on your inward condition than upon your outward circumstances. This inward condition has the qualities of meekness and mercy, is pure in heart and poor in spirit, and is sensitive toward men and single-minded toward God; then Jesus goes on to pronounce a beatitude upon those persons who bring healing to those splits which rend the harmony of life. "Blessed are the peacemakers," he says, "for they shall be called sons of God." In this chapter we make it our business to find the meaning of this ancient word of God for you and me in this day of our Lord.

I

The best way to begin is to look at that word "peacemakers." It is a double word, and the first part of it is "peace." In Greek it is *eirēnē*, from which we get our word irenic; and when you say of a man that he has an irenic nature, you mean he is a peace-loving man. But the Hebrew is much more interesting. It is *shalom*. When you walk down the street in Jerusalem or in Tel Aviv and see people meeting each other, their greeting is always "Shalom!" You get so used to the word that, even though you are an American, when you go into a shop to buy a package of tobacco you find yourself saying to the shopkeeper, "Shalom." The word means peace; and so in the land of Israel, when you greet a person you do not say to him, "Good morning"; you say "Shalom," "Peace be unto you." You can always remember the meaning of the word "Jerusalem" by noting that the second half of it is this same word: Jeru-shalom, Jerusalem. The word itself means "secure habitation," or "foundation of peace."

Furthermore, the quality which it signifies is a positive thing. It is never simply a negative state, never only the absence of trouble. Sometimes peace in a home is nothing more than an armed truce. Sometimes peace among nations is a mere armistice, a cessation of hostilities. But *shalom* always means everything that makes for the highest good. So when a man meets his friend on the street in Jerusalem and says to him "Shalom," he does not mean that he wishes for him only the absence of evil things; instead, he wishes for him the presence of all good things. When Jesus greeted his friends in the Upper Room following the Resurrection and said to them "Shalom," he was not simply wishing for them freedom from all trouble but rather the enjoyment of all good.

Notice also that Jesus did not say "Blessed are the peace-lovers." He said "Blessed are the peace-makers." To have a peaceable disposition is only half the job: the emphasis falls on the second part, bringing about peace between enemies. It speaks not only of those who keep the peace but of those who make the peace. A peacemaker is more than one who refuses to disturb the peace; it is the man who exerts himself to make the peace. And because peace is more a positive than a negative thing, being a peacemaker is not simply burying hatchets but promoting the highest good of other people.

The governmental agency known as the Peace Corps is thus in the biblical tradition. For these men and women who have left home and gone to foreign countries are there not simply to settle squabbles: they spend their time teaching the ignorant, feeding the hungry, and healing the sick, and in more ways than one they bring a better life to the people in the lands where they labor.

Peace is a positive thing, and peacemaking is active participation in the promotion of peace.

II

So much for the *what* of the text; move on to
the *how*. God is called the "God of peace." Jesus
is called the "Prince of Peace." A peacemaker is
called a "son of God." What methods can you use
to fulfill that role? The answer of the New Testament is twofold.

First of all, you can help to keep the peace. "So far
as it depends upon you" says Paul, "live peaceably
with all." (Rom. 12:18.) In some homes, in some
offices, in some country clubs, in some churches,
there are people who have a perfect genius for
stirring up trouble. Wherever they find a little
fire burning, they take perfect delight in adding
fuel to the fire. They are like the man in the
proverb from the Bible:

> He who meddles in a quarrel not his own
> is like one who takes a passing dog
> by the ears. (Prov. 26:17.)

The dog sets up a howl, and a molehill is turned
into a mountain.

But fortunately there are also people of another
bent. The presiding officer in a Presbyterian
Church court is called a moderator; and happy
is that home, that business, that church where

there are those who have a moderating influence. They remember that "A soft answer turns away wrath" (Prov. 15:1). They know that it takes two to make a quarrel. They are always on the lookout to find ways of pouring oil on troubled waters. "The difference between success and failure in our marriage," said one wife, "is that I refuse to say a half dozen things a day I feel like saying." The peacemaker keeps the peace by refusing to break the peace.

Epictetus was one of the wisest of the ancients, and he put the matter like this: "Every matter hath two handles. By the one it may be carried. By the other not. If thy brother do thee wrong take not this thing by the handle 'He wrongs me'; that is the handle by which it may not be carried. But take it by the handle 'He is my brother.' And thou wilt take it by the handle by which it may be carried easily."

In the early days of the Confederacy, General Robert E. Lee was criticized by General Whiting, and it would be a natural thing to suppose that Lee would wait for a time when he could return the compliment. Then a day came when President Davis called General Lee in and asked him what he thought of General Whiting. Without hesitation Lee commended Whiting in high terms and described him as one of the ablest men in the

Confederate army. An officer who was present motioned Lee aside and suggested that he must not know what unkind things Whiting had been saying about him. "I understood," said Lee, "that the President desired to know my opinion of Whiting, not Whiting's opinion of me."

There speaks the peacemaker who keeps the peace by refusing to break the peace. It is in the spirit of Jesus who counseled turning the other cheek and of his Apostle who describes love as something which "is patient and . . . bears all things." One method of the peacemaker is to keep the peace.

But of course anyone who reads the New Testament and sees it whole knows that along with keeping the peace, the peacemaker must sometimes disturb the peace. That sounds like double talk; but call it what you wish, and like it or not as you will, you cannot expunge it from the record. For the same Jesus who is called the Prince of Peace and who said "Peace I leave with you" said also, "Do not think that I have come to bring peace on earth; I have not come to bring peace, but a sword" (Matt. 10:34). The word "sword" here means division and dispeace; and he goes on to say further: "I have come to set a man against his father, and a daughter against her mother . . . , and a man's foes will be those of his own household" (Matt. 10:35-36).

That sounds like a contradiction, and the only way to resolve this paradox is to get back to the real meaning of peace. It is more than the absence of trouble: it is the possession of positive good when men are in right relation to God as their Father and, at the same time, in right relation to other men who are their brothers. It is more than tranquility. It is based on justice, or right relations. Nothing is ever settled until it is settled right. As long as there is injustice, as long as there are wrong relations between people, the person who is for peace at any price is no real peacemaker. When there is a boil on your body, you cannot cure it by rubbing salve on the spot; you've got to disturb the peace by lancing the thing and removing the cause of the trouble. When there is a boil on the body politic, you cannot cure it by letting well enough alone in the quiet of the status quo; you've got to disturb the peace by getting down to the root of the thing. So Jesus says: "Think not that I came to bring salve; I came not to bring salve but a sword"—a sword which, like the surgeon's knife, will lance the boil and remove the poison.

It is only in that light that we can understand in the least what is happening in our land today.

Like it or not—and most people who grew up in the South do not like it—we must admit that there has been a boil on the body politic. One hundred years ago the Negro was emancipated from his slavery, but not until now is he being liberated in his life. And the real cause of that liberation, and thus of the disturbance of our peace, is the gospel of Jesus Christ. You cannot tell a man that he is a child of God and expect him to be content forever with second-class citizenship. What is happening in America is akin to what is happening in the Congo and in other places: it is all a part of the same world revolution. And what is making it happen is that at last people are beginning to believe what the missionaries and the preachers have been telling them, namely, that in Christ there is neither bond nor free. The early disciples were described as those who "turned the world upside down" (Acts 17:6); and what you have today is a case of history repeating itself.

It is in this context that you must view the recent actions of certain church bodies in the area of civil rights. Likening demonstrations to the American Revolution of the founding fathers, one of them said this: "The Christian should recognize peaceful demonstrations as proper attempts to extend the right to fuller participation in the responsibilities and privileges of public life and, therefore, a more complete sense of human dignity." As for the sit-in, where it does not involve a breach of the law of trespass but is used to extend human dignity and increase respect, it should "receive his support."

But it is in the matter of civil disobedience that some are disturbed by the action of the churches. In seeking an understanding, you should remember certain truths. For example, the Constitution of my own church says three things. It says, first of all, that the state is instituted by God and therefore its law must be obeyed. It says that the officers of the state are duty bound to protect all the people from any indignity, violence, abuse, or injustice. And it says furthermore that "God alone is Lord of the conscience."

Then it takes these three facts and molds them into this guideline: When the protection of the law breaks down, a citizen whose conscience is ruled by the Holy Spirit and the Scriptures has a right to disobey the civil establishment. But it sets up this warning: "He should be very cautious about taking such a lonely position and should hold it only in fear and trembling," and "must recognize his liability to the judgment of the civil court." And the church should "give the support of Christian compassion" to any such member.

What it seems to me to be saying is this: That just as the conscientious objector in wartime disobeys the draft law because, like the early apostles, he must obey God rather than men, and his action is understood and accepted by the church; so the Christian who is led by his conscience to civil disobedience is entitled to the same Christian compassion.

When the church speaks in such fashion, it does so in the tradition of its Lord; for the peacemaker is one who not only keeps the peace but who disturbs the status quo, in the name of a higher peace.

III

So much for what peace means and how the peacemaker does his work. Move on now and notice that Jesus pronounces a beatitude upon him: "Blessed are the peacemakers, for they shall be called sons of God."

This is a typical Hebrew expression. The language is not rich in adjectives, and often when it wishes to describe something it uses not an adjective but the phrase "son of" plus an abstract noun. So a man may be called a son of peace instead of a peaceful man. Barnabas, you remember, is called a son of consolation instead of a comforting and encouraging man. Whenever you see a child do something which reminds you of his father, you say "That child is certainly a son of his father." What you mean is that he is like his father and so bears a family resemblance.

To be a son of God is to be like God, and to be godlike is to bear a family resemblance. The peacemaker is a son of God, for there is no more godlike work in all the world than peacemaking.

Wherever you find a spirit like that, whether in the church, or in industry, or in politics, or in the home, or in personal relationship, you have a person who is rightly named a son of God. And you will know the ways in which that calling presents its challenge to you.

8. Blessed Are Those Who Are Persecuted

"Blessed are those who are persecuted for righteousness' sake, for theirs is the kingdom of heaven."—Matthew 5:10

In this chapter we bring to a close our study of the Beatitudes, and the last one speaks of people whose goodness gets them into trouble: "Blessed are those who are persecuted for righteousness' sake," says Jesus, "for theirs is the kingdom of heaven."

This word makes you think immediately of the early days of the church. Our Lord himself was "persecuted for righteousness' sake" by being nailed to a cross. Of his twelve disciples only one, as far as we can tell, died in his bed, and several met death in the manner of their Master. In Jerusalem the authorities hounded the Christians unmercifully, and a young man named Saul breathed out "threatenings and slaughter" against them. In Rome this kind of thing went on for three hundred years. Followers of the Galilean were thrown to the lions and burned at the stake. Nero is said to have wrapped them in pitch, set them on fire, and used them as living torches to light his gardens. He even sewed them up in skins of wild animals and set his hunting dogs on them to tear them to death.

Anyone who knows his history knows that this beatitude has had its meaning in days gone by. Even in the early days of the American colonies a man was put in jail for preaching for no other reason than that he was a Presbyterian. But time marches on and tolerance becomes a virtue, and Thomas Jefferson writes his statute on religious freedom. It has been many a year since anyone has been burned at the stake for being a Christian or jailed for being a heretic. Is it possible that progress has made this beatitude obsolete and rendered irrevelant these words of Jesus? What meaning can it possibly have for people such as ourselves who live in this enlightened twentieth century?

I

As we seek to work our way into its significance, notice, first of all, that the promise of blessedness cannot be claimed by everybody who meets criticism and opposition. The fact of persecution in and of itself is no guarantee of happiness. The promise is limited by the words "for righteousness' sake." Billy Graham has written a book on the Beatitudes, and I found him saying this: "I have known professed Christians who were dominated by bad dispositions, snap judgments, and poor manners and thought that people were opposed to them because of their 'righteousness.' It was not their goodness which people resented—it was their lack of it."

Ralph Sockman makes a good point. He suggests that here we have a possible reason why Matthew lists this as the last of the Beatitudes. Before you conclude, he says, that you are being persecuted for your righteousness, you should study yourself in the light of the preceding qualities that are described. Are you sufficiently selfless to be called "poor in spirit"? Are you penitent for your sins, and do you share sympathetically in the sufferings of others? Is your meekness equal to a humility which gives first place to the will of God? Are you merciful to the needy, and do you hunger and thirst after goodness? Is your heart pure in the sense that you have a single-minded loyalty to God? Are you a peacemaker, pouring oil on troubled waters, or are you a peacebreaker, adding fuel to the fire? Are you reviled because you have been good at reviling? And do people speak evil of you because you have a tongue given to gossip and to talebearing and bearing false witness? When we put questions like these to ourselves, we have to admit sometimes that it is not our virtues but our faults which are responsible for criticism and opposition; and we are disliked not for our goodness but for our lack of it.

II

Nevertheless, there are people who are persecuted for righteousness' sake, for the simple reason that the spirit of Christ has not yet conquered the world sufficiently to make persecution a thing of the past; and the last beatitude has a relevance for us just at it had for those early Christians who met opposition.

You begin to see the truth when you put together two facts which are as clear as the nose on your face. The first is that there is warfare going on in this world. In the last chapter we talked about the peacemaker who fulfills his role in two ways. First of all, he keeps the peace. "So far as it depends upon you," says Paul, "live peaceably with all." But, second, not only does he keep the peace, but there are times when, in order to be a peacemaker, he must disturb the peace. Notice that no sooner has Jesus pronounced a blessing upon the peacemaker than he comes right back with this word about persecution, to remind us that we are not expected to come to terms with every force which is at enmity with us. "Do not think that I have come to bring peace," he said elsewhere, "but a sword." "The kingdom of heaven," he said, "is like leaven which a woman . . . hid in three measures of meal" (Matt. 13:33). He had often seen it in his home—even as you have— fermenting, bubbling, making the dough rise and fall. The process of leavening the life of the world will always be like that: it will create unrest because there can never be peace between right and wrong.

That is the first fact: There is warfare going on in this world. The second is this: When you get into this struggle on the right side, you've got to expect trouble. This world being what it is and the basic principles of Christ being what they are and the contrast between the two being unmistakable, any genuine adherence to Christ is bound to bring on persecution. They may not burn you at the stake any longer, but they will burn you in other ways. They may not put you on a cross literally, but they will crucify you socially or financially or politically. They may not stone you with stones, but they will pound you with anonymous letters and telephone calls and slanders. They will revile you, and persecute you, and say all manner of evil against you falsely.

You have heard Professor T. R. Glover quoted before, but his word comes to mind at this point. He said that Jesus promised three things to his followers. First, they would be entirely fearless: "Fear not." Second, they would be absurdly happy: "My joy I give unto you." And finally, they would always be in trouble: "In the world you have tribulation." And who is there who has tried to be loyal to his Christian conscience and has not found this last to be true?

Here, for example, is a girl who in her home or at some church meeting catches a view of the vision splendid and sets herself to follow the gleam. She remembers the commandments and refuses to allow herself to be made a plaything for the pleasure of her male companions, and what do they do? They call her a prude, and tell her she will lose her popularity and grow up to be a wallflower.

Here is a young man who hears the voice of God telling him that his place of work is in the ministry or on the mission field. When he makes that fact known, he must endure the scorn of his friends and the ill-concealed disappointment of his family. When Albert Schweitzer turned his back on a brilliant career in medicine and music and teaching and decided to go to Africa, he spoke of the "many verbal duels" he had to fight with relatives and friends who argued with him over the folly of his enterprise.

Here is a young couple who have a conscience on certain matters. When they do not entertain according to accepted patterns, they find themselves eliminated from the invitation lists of their friends. Here is a businessman who cannot go along with the policies of his company, and before long discovers his services are no longer needed. Here is a minister whom I knew in Little Rock, who follows the law of the land and the doctrine of his denomination and the dictates of his conscience about open schools; and then is waited upon by the officers of his church and told that he must move on because the effectiveness of his ministry in that place has come to an end. And of course the ministers are not the only persons who know the criticism and opposition which come from taking the side of justice.

No, the day of persecution for the Christian has not come to an end. As a matter of fact, one writer claims that if we lack knowledge of the meaning of this beatitude, it may be because we are lacking in loyalty. And another goes so far as to say that persecution is a test as to whether your Christianity is alive. For it was none other than Jesus himself who said this: "Woe to you, when all men speak well of you" (Luke 6:26).

Iona is an island off the western coast of Scotland where Christianity was planted fourteen hundred years ago and from which the Presbyterian fatherland of Scotland was evangelized. In 1938, Sir George MacLeod, a minister, began there the work of the Iona community for the renewal of the church. It was twelve years ago in Austin, Texas, that I first met him; and something he said then has stayed in my mind ever since. His concern about the church, he said, was that there was nothing about it which made the world want to crucify it.

If persecution is the test of a live Christianity, then he is very nearly right; but it could be that the criticisms we read about are signs of a new life.

III

The text has a third thing to say to us. Notice that the Beatitudes begin with the word "blessed," which means happy, and they end with the word "rejoice," which means be glad. There is a spirit of buoyancy which throbs through all these sayings and which is especially characteristic of the last. Sometimes, when folks criticize you for your brand of goodness, you may feel tempted to develop a martyr complex and find your satisfaction in a morbid self-pity. But Jesus says you are "blessed" when others revile you and persecute you. You are to "rejoice" and be exceedingly glad; and then he goes on and lists certain reasons why you are entitled to a certain gladness when your goodness gets you into trouble.

For one thing, you can have the satisfaction of knowing that you are doing something for him. When your persecution is "for my sake" or "on my account," you are counting for something and having a share in the victory he is out to win. When the fight for religious freedom was going on in England, a man named Hugh Latimer was burned at stake, and this is what he said to his companion in martyrdom: "Be of good comfort, Master Ridley, and play the man; we shall this day light such a candle by God's grace in England as I trust shall never be put out." It is written of Jesus that he endured the cross "for the joy that was set before him." Criticism and opposition assumed voluntarily for Christ are the Christian's cross; and when it is borne for his sake and on his account, it wins a share of his joy.

At the 1948 Olympic games in London a dramatic incident occurred. In a relay race the French team started well, but as the baton was being passed, one of the runners dropped it. The accident put the team out of the race, and the runner at fault fell to the ground and cried like a baby. Your life does not begin with your birth nor end with your death. Society, said Edmund Burke, is a compact between the living, the dead, and the great unborn. To keep faith with those who have gone before and those who come after is the business of the Christian; and for his sake to pass on the torch is to know the satisfaction of helping him to win the race.

There is something else which goes into this cup of joy, and that is the knowledge that you are doing your duty. I take this way of putting the promise which Jesus pledges to the persecuted: "For theirs," he says, "is the kingdom of heaven." The kingdom of heaven is the rule of the will of God, and the will of God is what gives a man his duty. When in spite of criticism and opposition you see your duty in the light of your loyalty to the will of God and do it, then yours will be the satisfaction which nothing on earth can give or take away. For I ask you: Do you know any deeper joy than the knowledge of duty done? H. H. Farmer knew what he was talking about when he defined true blessedness as "doing God's will and in the fellowship with him such doing brings."

Jesus lists a third source of happiness. "Rejoice," he said, "and be glad. . . . For so men persecuted the prophets who were before you." It is the joy of sharing a noble tradition and belonging to a great and goodly company. When I was in grade school, our family lived next door to the campus of Louisana State University in Baton Rouge. We boys used to spend the afternoons on the baseball field, watching the team practice. We got to know the players, and when a game was on they graciously allowed us to file through the players' gate with them, carrying a mitt or a mask or a bat. Of course it was nice getting in without having to buy a ticket, but the greater pleasure came from the pride of feeling that we were identified with the players and were somehow a part of the team. Think of being on the same team with Isaiah and Jeremiah and Elijah and Paul and Simon and Polycarp and Hugh Latimer. When your goodness gets you into trouble, says Jesus, "Rejoice . . . . For so men persecuted the prophets who were before you." You belong to that goodly company.

Finally, he says, your gladness is enhanced by the knowledge that "your reward is great in heaven." Of course the whole question of rewards

107

is a ticklish one, because it is so easy to turn motive into selfish desire and to be a Christian only for what you can get out of it. Yet some reward there must be, or life would be robbed of its meaning. There must be a different result for the life which shows loyalty and the life which lacks it, or else this world would be a place of "sound and fury, signifying nothing." That word "result" is the key. In the Bible, rewards are not so much rewards as results; and the result of taking up a cross for his sake is the privilege of sharing a long future of fellowship with him who, when he was reviled, reviled not again.

Billy Graham writes that he has a friend who during the depression lost a job, a fortune, a wife, and a home—but he held onto a faith in the eternal goodness of things. One day he stopped to watch some men cutting stone for a huge church; one of them was chiseling a triangular piece of rock. "What are you doing with that?" the spectator asked. "See that little opening away up there near the spire?" said the workman. "Well, I'm shaping this down here so it will fit up there." As the man walked away, he heard a voice: "I'm shaping you down here so you'll fit in up there."

When your goodness gets you into trouble, "Rejoice and be glad." The stones of persecution will become precious stones and will shine like stars in your crown.

I know people who say that this last beatitude is the most meaningful of all for them, and I trust that our study may give it meaning for you.